Contents

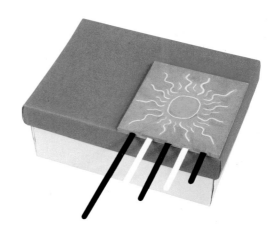

All about musical instruments

People have used musical instruments for thousands of years to make tuneful and rhythmic sounds. They are played in many different ways all over the world.

TYPES OF INSTRUMENT

There are four different groups of musical instrument: percussion, string, wind and keyboard.

Percussion instruments, such as drums and cymbals, can be hit, clashed together, shaken or even scraped to produce a sound.

String instruments (see left), such as the violin and harp, give out a sound from their strings when played with a bow or plucked with the fingers. The strings are stretched over a hollow wooden box which makes the sound louder.

Wind instruments, including the flute and trumpet (see below), are tubes made from wood or metal that the player blows into. This is sometimes through a reed, or by vibrating the lips, like blowing a raspberry, into a mouthpiece.

Keyboard instruments, such as the piano and synthesizer, use sets of keys, levers and buttons which are pressed down to hammer out a note.

Musical Instruments

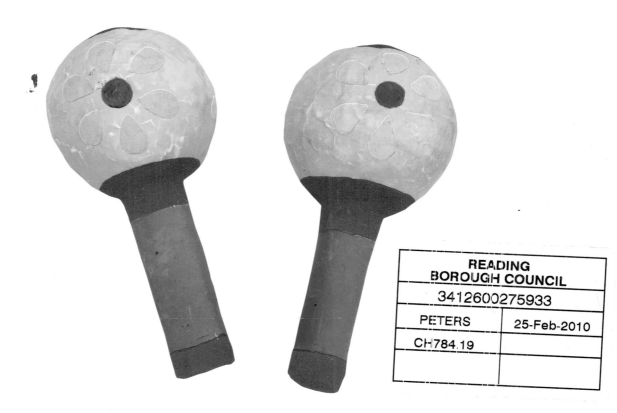

Anna-Marie D'Cruz

Reading Borough Council

First published in 2007
by Wayland

This paperback edition published in 2010
by Wayland

© Copyright 2007 Wayland

Wayland
338 Euston Road
London NW1 3BH

Wayland Australia
Level 17/207 Kent Street
Sydney NSW 2000

Senior Editor: Jennifer Schofield
Designer: Jason Billin
Project maker: Anna-Marie D'Cruz
Photographer: Chris Fairclough
Proofreader: Susie Brooks

Acknowledgements:
The Publisher would like to thank the following models:
Emel Augustin, Jade Campbell, Ammar Duffus, Akash Kohli,
Ellie Lawrence, Adam Menditta, Eloise Ramplin, Robin Stevens.

Picture Credits:
Alll photography by Chris Fairclough except for
pages 2, 4, 8 bottom left Hachette Children's books;
page 5 top Lindsay Hebberd/CORBIS; page 7 bottom
right Pete Saloutos/CORBIS

CIP data
D'Cruz, Anna-Marie
    Musical instruments. - (Make and use)
    1. Musical instruments - Construction - Juvenile literature
    I. Title
    784.1'923

ISBN: 9780750261678

Printed in China

Wayland is a division of Hachette Children's Books,
an Hachette UK Company.
www.hachette.co.uk

Note to parents and teachers:
The projects in this book are designed to be made by children. However, we recommend adult supervision at all times as the Publisher cannot be held responsible for any injury caused while making the projects.

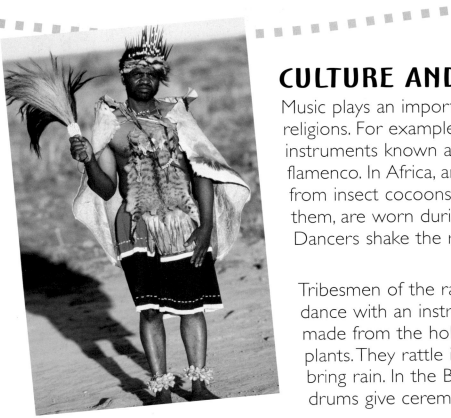

CULTURE AND MUSIC

Music plays an important role in many cultures and religions. For example, Spanish dancers use instruments known as castanets while dancing the flamenco. In Africa, ankle rattles, sometimes made from insect cocoons with seeds or stones inside them, are worn during tribal dances (see left). Dancers shake the rattles to add rhythm.

Tribesmen of the rainforests in South America dance with an instrument called the rainmaker, made from the hollow stems of dried cactus plants. They rattle it to call on the gods to bring rain. In the Buddhist religion, bells and drums give ceremonies a rythmic beat.

GET STARTED!

In this book you can discover ways of making interesting musical instruments from around the world. Try to use materials that you already have either at home or at school. For example, for the cardboard in these projects, the backs of used-up notepads, writing pads, art pads and hardbacked envelopes are ideal. Reusing and recyling materials like this is good for the environment and it will save you money. The projects have all been made and decorated for this book but do not worry if yours look a little different — just have fun making and playing your instruments.

Spanish castanets

Castanets are percussion instruments that are held in the hand. They are used in flamenco dancing to tap out a rhythm. Can you click out your own rhythm with these fun castanets?

YOU WILL NEED

piece of coloured card, 15cm x 8cm

2 buttons about 4cm wide

pencil

pair of scissors

coloured paper

glue

50cm cord

masking tape

sticky pads

1 Fold the card in half. Put a button in the centre of one side of the card. Draw the shape shown around it, making sure the circular part is wider than the button. With the card still folded, cut out the shape but do not cut along the fold.

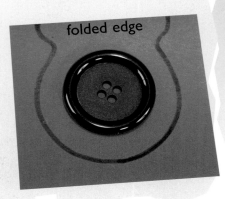

folded edge

2 Cut out shapes from the coloured paper and glue them on to the outside of the castanets.

3 Tie a double knot at each end of the cord. Stick the middle of the cord to the inside of the fold with masking tape.

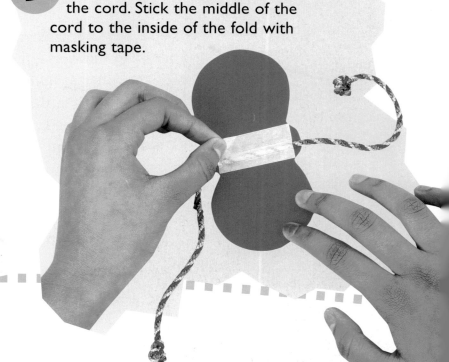

4 Tie the cord around the fold as shown. Remember, it needs to be loose enough to fit two fingers under it.

5 Use the sticky pads to attach buttons to the insides of the castanets.

6 Your castanets are now ready to play. Slip your first two fingers between the cord and the castanets. Then use your fingers to knock the two halves together against your palm. How fast can you click them?

GET DANCING!

Flamenco dancers hold a set of castanets in each hand. Those in the right hand have a higher sound or pitch and are known as hembra (female). The castanets in the left hand are lower in pitch and are called macho (male).

Simple flute

The flute is a wind instrument, so notes are made by blowing into it. This flute is easy to make and does not need many materials. When you have made it, try blowing out your favourite tunes.

YOU WILL NEED

4 strips of paper, each 3cm x 8cm

masking tape

2 clean long lollipop sticks

greaseproof paper

coloured tape

1 Fold each strip of paper in half longways three times to make a small block.

2 Tape two blocks of paper the same distance in from either end of one of the lollipop sticks. Now do the same for the other stick.

WIND POWER

The first wind instruments were made from animal bones with holes down the side, a bit like today's recorders. Since then, wind instruments have been made from wood and metal.

3 Cut a rectangle of greaseproof paper that is twice the width of the sticks and long enough to cover the paper blocks. Fold it in half along the longest length.

4 Place a lollipop stick in front of you with the paper blocks facing upward. Lay the strip of greaseproof paper on top of the stick and tape it to the ends of the stick. Make sure the greaseproof paper is as straight and as tight as possible.

5 Lay the second lollipop stick on top of the other stick with the paper blocks facing downwards. Wrap some tape around both lollipop sticks to hold everything together.

6 Blow through the sticks with the folded edge of greaseproof paper towards you. This makes the surfaces of the greaseproof paper vibrate, producing a noise. If you gently squeeze the sticks together as you blow, you can change the pitch of the note.

Bongo drums

Bongo drums are believed to have come from Cuba and are traditionally made from two different-sized drums. Make these colourful bongos and beat out your favourite song.

YOU WILL NEED

plastic carrier bag

pair of scissors

2 empty crisp tubes with no lids – different sizes if possible

permanent marker

masking tape

coloured paper

glue

2 strips of stiff cardboard 2cm wide and 4cm longer than the shorter tube

ruler

paint and paint brush

double-sided tape

1 Cut down one side and across the bottom of the carrier bag so that you have a single layer of plastic. Put a tube on the plastic and draw around it. Cut out the circle, adding an extra 5cm all around. Do the same for the second tube.

2 Place a circle of plastic over the open end of a tube. Using pieces of masking tape, stick the plastic down all around the side. Keep pulling the plastic tightly as you do this. Wrap another piece of tape around the tube to make sure the plastic is stuck firmly. Do the same with the second tube.

MAKE SOME NOISE!

The drums are different sizes so that they make different sounds. The sound a drum makes also depends on its shape, what it is made from and how tight the skin at the top of the drum is.

3 Cut a sheet of coloured paper large enough to go around each tube. Decorate it with different shapes and colours of paper. Wrap the decorated sheets around the tubes and glue them down.

4 Stick the two strips of cardboard together, end to end with each strip overlapping the other by 4cm.

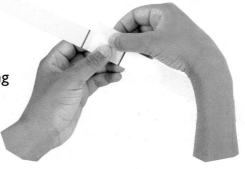

5 Fold up either side of the overlap and fix tape around the ends of the strips to form a triangle. Decorate the triangle by painting it. Stick the triangle to the tubes with double-sided tape, making sure the base of the triangle is at the top of the tubes.

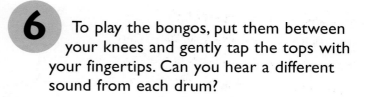

6 To play the bongos, put them between your knees and gently tap the tops with your fingertips. Can you hear a different sound from each drum?

Jazz washboard

Washboards were originally used for washing clothes. People doing their laundry noticed that the corrugated surface made a good sound when they scraped their fingers over it. Make a washboard and create some jazz!

1 Draw a line across the stiff card 3cm from the top. Then draw lines down the card, 3cm in from either side. Draw a line across the card 10cm from the bottom.

2 Draw another line 7cm from the bottom of the card and cut around it, making sure you are left with the shape shown.

3 Glue down the corrugated paper in the centre of your frame, making sure that the grooves go across the frame.

SPOONS, KAZOOS AND JUGS

Washboards are played by musicians in a jug band. Members of a jug band play instruments made from things found in the home, such as a jug, spoons and a kazoo. A kazoo is a comb covered in tissue paper that is blown across to make a tune. What other things from around your house could you use to make music?

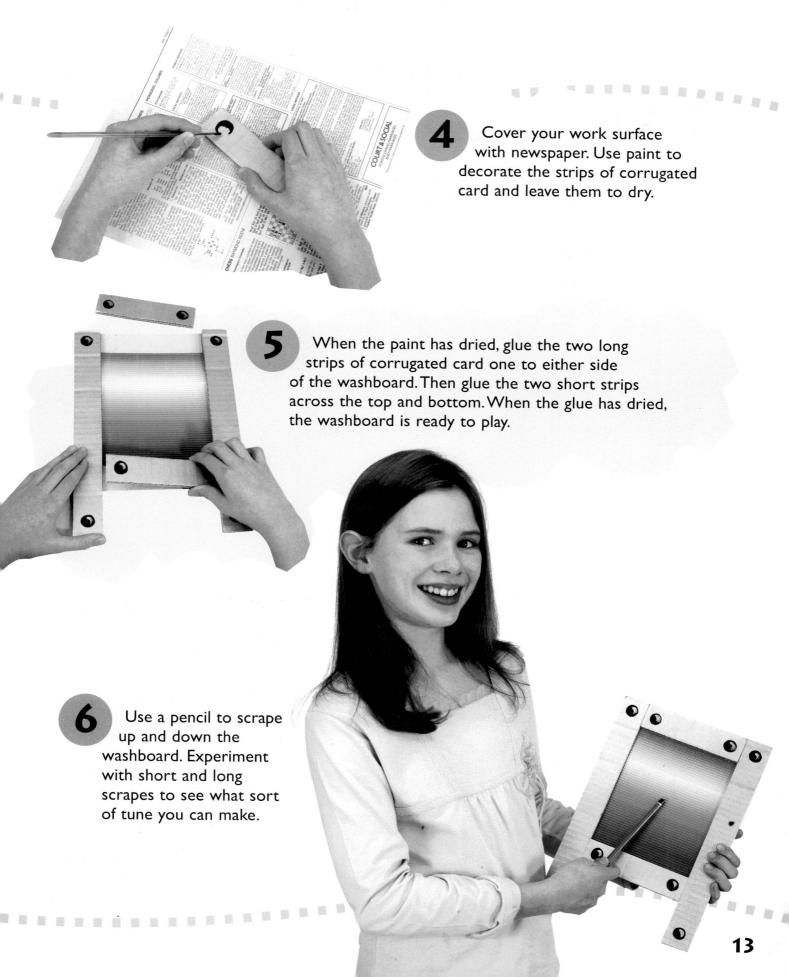

4 Cover your work surface with newspaper. Use paint to decorate the strips of corrugated card and leave them to dry.

5 When the paint has dried, glue the two long strips of corrugated card one to either side of the washboard. Then glue the two short strips across the top and bottom. When the glue has dried, the washboard is ready to play.

6 Use a pencil to scrape up and down the washboard. Experiment with short and long scrapes to see what sort of tune you can make.

African thumb piano

Thumb pianos are played by plucking keys. The keys are fixed to a wooden box or a hollowed gourd. Follow these steps to make a thumb piano and create a gentle melody.

1 Place one of the card squares down on your work surface. Arrange five of the stirrers so that they match those in the picture.

2 Glue the first stirrer down in place. Glue the next stirrer 1.5cm further out over the end of the card. Glue down the remaining stirrers, moving each one out another 1.5cm further than the previous one.

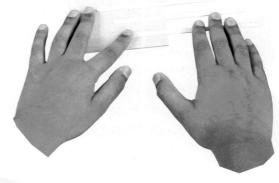

3 Measure out six 10-cm-long strips from the spare card, wide enough to fit the gaps between the stirrers. Cut them out and glue them onto the card between the stirrers.

4 Glue the other square of card over the top to cover the stirrers up and leave to dry.

Any sound we hear is a result of something moving. With the thumb piano, the quivering movement, known as vibration, of the plucked sticks makes the sound. Vibrations are made louder, or amplified, with the use of a hollow container, known as a soundbox.

5 Cover your work surface with newspaper. Paint the square. With the end of the spare wooden stirrer scratch a design into the square. Leave the square to dry. Then paint alternate keys black.

6 When all the paint has dried, place the piano on top of the shoe box which will act as a soundbox. Hold down the piano with one hand while you twang the keys with your fingers on the other. Experiment on different surfaces to see if you can create different sounds.

Hand drum

The chod drum is a small, double-sided hand drum. It is used by Buddhist monks during meditation. To play the drum, you need to twist your hand so that the knots swing from side to side, hitting the drumheads.

YOU WILL NEED

2 shoelaces, about 35cm long

empty cardboard cheese-triangle tub

stapler

masking tape

paint and paintbrush

pair of scissors

coloured card

glue

double-sided tape

1m length of wide ribbon

1 Staple one end of each lace onto the inside of the bottom of the tub. The laces need to be directly opposite each other. Stick a piece of tape over each staple.

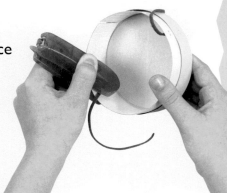

2 Cut each lace so that it reaches beyond the middle of the side of the drum. Make a knot at the end of each shoelace.

3 Put the lid back on the tub with the laces hanging on the outside of it. Tape the tub shut all the way around, taping over the laces.

4 Paint the rims of the tub and allow them to dry. Add a strip of coloured card around the side of the tub.

5 Cut circles of card big enough to cover the lid and bottom of the tub. Stick the card down and decorate it with shapes of coloured card.

6 Stick double-sided tape around the edge of the tub. Place the tub on your work surface with the lid facing upwards and the laces on the left and right.

7 Stick down the centre of the length of ribbon at the far side of the tub edge. Then stick the ribbon around the edge. Staple the ribbon together where the ends meet at the bottom.

8 The hand drum is now ready to play. Hold onto the ribbon, and place your fingertips at the bottom of the drum. Twist your wrist and watch the laces swing from side to side.

CHANTING MONKS

Buddhists are people who follow the religious beliefs of a man called Siddharta Gautama. Buddhist monks are men who give up their possessions and family to spend time studying holy books, chanting and meditating.

Shaking maracas

Maracas are popular in Latin America. They were originally made from hollowed-out gourds that had been left to dry. The steps below make one maraca, so you will need to repeat the instructions to make another one.

1 Begin by laying out sheets of newspaper over your work area. Blow up a balloon to the size you would like your maraca to be and knot it. Rest it on a beaker with the knotted part facing upwards.

2 To papier mâché the balloon, stick bits of newspaper with lots of the glue and water mixture onto the balloon. Leave a space around the knot. When you have built four layers over the balloon, go over it with a layer of white paper. Leave the balloon to dry.

3 When the balloon is dry, hold onto the knot and carefully pop the balloon with a pair of scissors. Remove any pieces of balloon stuck in the paper shell. Rest the shell on the beaker with the hole at the top. Use the funnel to pour in the rice.

4 To make a handle for the maraca, roll up the thin card into a tube. It must be big enough to sit over the hole of the ball and long enough for you to hold.

5 Fix the handle together using a stapler. Then snip a short way up around one end of the tube. Fan the snipped bits out. Sit the fanned end over the hole in the ball and stick it down with pieces of tape. Tape up the other end of the handle.

6 Papier mâché the handle with a few layers of white paper.

7 While the handle is drying, make the second maraca by repeating steps one to six. When both are completely dry, paint the maracas with brightly coloured patterns. When the paint is dry, have a dance and shake your maracas.

GET CRAFTY!

Papier mâché is a way of creating shapes from paper and a glue mixture, which when dry, are hard and can be painted. Your mixture of PVA glue and water should be more runny than glue but not watery. Try adding the water a teaspoon at a time to make sure you do not add too much water.

Egyptian harp

Harps were played in Ancient Egypt. They came in many different shapes and sizes. Some had only a few strings while others had more than 20. This Egyptian harp takes time to make, but it is well worth it!

1 Take the lid off the shoe box. Cut a slit just over halfway down the middle of one end of the box, as wide as the edge of the hanger.

2 Mark four points down the middle length of the top of the lid. Push through a paper fastener at each point and open it up on the underside. Put the lid back onto the box and tape around it to seal the box. Do not tape over the slit.

3 Using the picture as a guide, draw an animal's head on the coloured card. Draw the neck slightly longer so that you can stick it to the box. Cut out the head and decorate it. Decorate the rest of the box.

EGYPTIANS AND MUMMIES

Animals were very important to the Ancient Egyptians. They believed that some animals had supernatural powers. Often when the animals died, they were mummified, so that they could be buried with their owners.

4 Make a 1-cm slit at the bottom of the head to make tabs. Bend the tabs in opposite directions. Stick the head to the end of the box without the slit with double-sided tape.

5 Ask an adult to help you to remove the hook from the coathanger. Using strong tape, stick an elastic band onto the centre of the hanger. Tape on three more elastic bands as shown.

6 Ask an adult to help you with this step. Push the end of the hanger without the elastic bands into the slit at the back of the box. Rest it on the bottom of the box. While holding the hanger up, stretch the lowest elastic band to hook it onto nearest fastener. Repeat with the other elastic bands, each time moving up the hanger and hooking onto the next fastener.

7 The harp is now ready to play. Either rest it on a table or place it between your knees and pluck the elastic bands. Can you play a gentle tune?

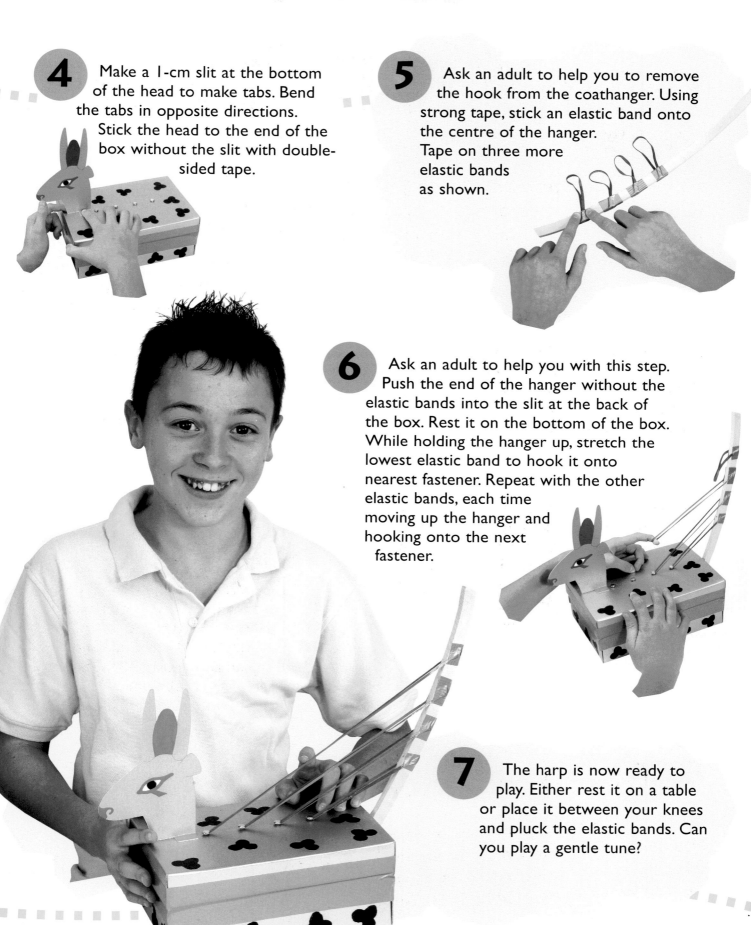

Glossary

amplify

To amplify sounds is to make them stronger or louder. On a thumb piano, the soundbox amplifies the sound.

Buddhists

People who follow the teachings or religious beliefs of Siddharta Gautama.

chanting

Saying or calling words out in a special rhythm. Some religions, such as Buddhism, use chanting as a way to pray.

drumheads

The part of the drum that you beat against, often with your hand or a stick.

flamenco

A type of dance done mainly in Spain. Flamenco dancers use castanets to tap out the rhythmn of their dance.

gourd

The hard skin of a fruit. The skin is hollowed out and dried to make musical instruments.

keyboard instruments

Musical instruments that have levers, pedals and keys that are pushed or pressed to create a note. Pianos and organs are keyboard instruments.

Latin America

Parts of Central and South America where Spanish and Portuguese are the main languages spoken.

meditating

To meditate is to think deeply and seriously about something. Some religions use meditation as a type of prayer.

monks

Holy men that live in monasteries.

mummify

To treat a body with oils and wrap it in cloth to preserve it once it has been burried.

papier mâché

Paper that has been made into a pulp or layered with a glue and water mixture to make objects that are solid when dry.

percussion instruments

Musical instruments that are shaken, beaten, hit together or scraped to make a sound. Drums are a type of percussion instrument.

pitch

How low or high a voice or musical note sounds. Men usually have low-pitched voices and women have high-pitched voices.

recycling

To recycle something is to change it or treat it so that it can be used again.

soundbox

The hollow part of a string instrument that amplifies the sound, making it louder or stronger.

string instruments

Musical instruments that have strings that need to be plucked, pulled or combed to make a sound. Guitars, harps and cellos are all string instruments.

vibrations

Vibrations happen when something moves to and fro very quickly. This makes a quivering sound.

wind instruments

Musical instruments that are blown or sucked to make a sound. Flutes and recorders are wind instruments.

FURTHER INFORMATION

www.usd.edu/smm/galleries.html
The website for the National Music Museum at the University of South Dakota, USA. It has lots of pictures of many different types of instruments.

www.ram.ac.uk/museum
The website for the Royal Academy of Music Museum in London, United Kingdom has information and pictures of historical and modern musical instruments.

www.dsokids.com/2001/instrumentchart.htm
This interactive website has a chart of the different orchestral instruments to see and hear.

www.town4kids.com/town4kids/kids/music4kids/world/worldmap.htm
This website has all the facts on musical instruments from around the world. There are also audio-clips to listen to.

Note to parents and teachers:

The website addresses (URLs) included in this book were valid at the time of going to press. However, because of the nature of the Internet, it is possible that some addresses may have changed, or sites may have changed or closed down since publication. While the authors and publishers regret any inconvenience this may cause the readers, no responsibility for any such changes can be accepted by either the authors or the publisher.

Index